ANCIENT EGYPT

Legends. Gods. Pharaohs.

THE HISTORY HOUR

CONTENTS

❦ I ❧
INTRODUCTION

❦❧

This is the story of a long-lived Ancient Egyptian Civilization. The dates herein may differ from those in other texts, because Ancient Egypt used differing methods of chronology. In addition, many of the narrations in this book are derived from the hieroglyphics and variations occur depending upon the translator.

❦❧

Ancient Egypt was a fortress to belief and beauty that will forever stand as a testimonial to the human spirit. It had it great pharaohs, as well as the negligent and tired ones. There were male and female pharaohs...There were White pharaohs, Brown pharaohs and Black pharaohs – all heralding from within their own borders. Ancient Egypt was a blended civilization. Inside this book, there are stories gleaned from the tales of great conquests and the lives of the priests, scribes and ordinary Egyptian toiling amidst the waters of the Nile River. There are stories here about mummification and the hidden mysteries as well. Those with an ear for secrets will ferret them out. Ancient Egypt was a land of magic and awesome wonder.

❧ II ❧
THE GODS GUIDE ME

❦

"I developed myself from the primeval matter which I made. My name is 'Osiris,' the germ of primeval matter."

❦

It was said in the ancient papyri that, if you know the name of a god or devil and addressed him by his name, he had to respond. If you wished, he could bring down a curse upon whomever you wished it. Or if you wanted to bring upon the other a blessing, it would be done. Such was the spiritual and worldly power of the ancient Egyptians. Ancient Egypt lasted for 2000 years, so perhaps it was a formidable power indeed. Now, there is a caveat to possessing such great power. In order to gain the power of a god, you need to know its name.

The stories of creation, fratricide and resurrection have been told and retold according to the beliefs of millions of people world-wide from time immemorial. There were two founders of Ancient Rome, Romulus and Remus who were brothers. Romulus killed Remus in the course of an argument – the first fratricide. In the Judeo-Christian texts, Cain killed his brother Abel. And in the Papyrus of Turin, that is part of a hieroglyphic history of Ancient Egypt, *Set* killed *Osiris,* who was his brother. He did this by giving *Osiris* poison from a cobra. *Osiris'* sister and also his wife, *Isis,* plunged into deep despair. If only she knew the name of the god who had the power of resurrection, he could be reborn! There was great power in a divine name. Isis cried to whomever was the heavenly father, pleading with him to surrender his name. After taking pity upon her, the god responded:

> *"I have made the heavens, I have stretched out the two horizons like a curtain, and I have placed the soul of the gods within them. I am He who, if He opens his eye, makes the light, and, if He closes them, darkness comes into being. At my command the Nile rises. I create the days. I create the Nile flood. I am* **Ra.***"*

ᘒᘒᘒ

Then *Isis* rushed to the body of her husband, *Osiris,* and called upon the name of **Ra** to rid *Osiris* of the poison and bring him back to life. And so it was.

MAKING PAPYRUS: A
PAINSTAKING PROCESS

෴

The above story was recorded on papyrus. Papyrus is made from a sedge grass called *Cyperus papyrus*. Imagine trying to re-glue paper after it's been shredded. The artisan first removes the outer coating of a green stem, scoops out its fibrous interior and then flattens it, after which he glues the thin strips together.

෴

In the Old Kingdom (2686-2181 BC), the Egyptians had magnificent craftsmen, some of whom were employed full-time in making glue! It was made mostly from boiling animal hides along with the fat and gristle – certainly a dirty process. After the mixture cooled significantly, it was strained until the substance was free of particulates. Then it was painted, again flattened, and cut into sheets. Sometimes resins from woody trees was used.

꧁꧂

Inks and paints were made from powdered minerals that were mixed with water.

THE STORIES ON THE PAPYRI

✦

Authors of the texts were priests or magicians, who related the stories of the gods who were responsible for bringing life to the earth. They were intended to be informational, entertaining and educational. History was told in the form of these stories. Always, the role of the deities in everyone's life was highlighted. People felt as if they were going through their lives side-by-side with these gods, as if they were specters or ghosts. The gods helped them cope with their feelings; the gods punished them for bad behavior; the gods sometimes ignored them. The gods were like them. They were capable of valor or evil. They acted in very human ways, but possessed super-human powers. That could be a problem and a cause of disasters – natural and otherwise.

✦

THE CAST OF CHARACTERS IN
THE LEGENDS

The Main Gods:

෨෯෨

Introductory Note

As stories about the gods were told and retold through the centuries, there are differences that can be noted. On occasion, the names are different and the portrayals likewise differ. Every teller of the tale retold it, and with his own creativity altered the names and the tales somewhat. These legends were circulated in the two kingdoms of Egypt, the Upper and Lower Kingdoms and were carried to Greece and even Mesopotamia. Therefore, there are different translations involved. In addition, the history and myths were related verbally until they could be painted or inscribed, so there were variations that crept in. Thus, the names used below may appear slightly different than in other accounts. At any rate, the meanings of the aspects of the stories bear recognizable similarities. One needs to interpret liberally.

NUN or NU

Nun is the chaos of the beginning of time. It is the primordial waters from which life came forth. It was the universe before the "Big Bang."

RA or AMON

Ra is the sun.

> *The Rising sun, also called Khepera*
> *The Sun at noon, also called Ra*
> *The Sun in the evening, also called Temu*

MUT

The deity *Mut* was the wife of *Amon*. She was the primeval earth mother who was self-created from the primordial waters. Her name didn't come into popular use as a deity until the Middle and Late Kingdoms.

TEFNUT and SHU

Tefnut is the daughter of *Ra and Mut*. She is symbolized by the rain, and the moisture in the sky (clouds). It was said that she once ran away from her palace to Nubia (current-day Sudan) and *Thoth*, the god of wisdom, had to go after her to bring her home to her parents. Upon analysis, one can see the relationship between the departure of the rain and the dry period following the annual Nile flood. *Tefnut* is often portrayed on the frescoes as holding two cobras to signify her divine power. She married her brother *Shu*. Of course, they were the only two gods then, so that was necessary in order to produce offspring.

❧

Shu was *Tefnut's* spouse. *Shu* is symbolized by air or the wind. It was his duty to separate the skies above from the earth below. Likewise, he was tasked with managing the space between the sky and the ground. It is interesting to note here that young children often color the sky along the top of a paper, and the ground along the bottom, leaving a space in between. It is within that space that humans, trees and animals are drawn.

❧

In hieroglyphics, *Shu* is often portrayed as an ostrich feather. The feather is bent, as if it's blowing in the wind. Sometimes *Shu* is associated with a parched earth, to represent a period of aridity causing famine. In that sense, he is the paternal figure who is disciplining his children.

❧

NUT and GEB

Nut, the daughter of *Telmut* and *Shu,* is the sky of the day and the evening sky at night studded with stars. Sometimes she was portrayed in the hieroglyphics as a cow suckling her young, the people.

❧

Geb, is the son of *Telmut* and *Shu,* is the earth. He was sometimes pictured in hieroglyphics as a goose, or a seated pharaoh. Occasionally, he has two vipers encircling his head, signifying his power. When a figure is seen in the frescoes with a goose on his head, it symbolizes the power of a pharaoh of the two Egypts – the Upper Kingdom, which is seen in Southern Egypt on a map, and the Lower Kingdom, which encompasses the delta region of the Nile River as it leads from the Mediterranean Sea.

Nut and *Geb* had four children – *Isis, Osiris, Nepthys, Horus the Elder* and *Set.*

ISIS

Isis, about whom the earlier tale was told, is considered the mother-goddess. She gives life to children through childbirth and nurture. She brings food and nourishment and is compassionate and loving. *Isis* is a great protector, demonstrating the maternal instinct of protecting her children like a lioness protects her cubs.

In the frescoes, she has a block-like crown, signifying Upper and Lower Egypt. *Isis* is a powerful goddess and has pharaonic powers. In hieroglyphics, she is portrayed by her crown or a seated pharaoh queen. Frequently, she is pictured with her divine child, *Horus.*

OSIRIS

Osiris is married to *Isis* and is one of chief gods of Ancient Egypt. As the god of the dead, it is he who ministers to the soul (called *ka*) of the recently departed. *Osiris* guides one's soul in the difficult journey to the afterlife of glory and into the rebirth into the new self. *Osiris* lived a mortal life prior to his becoming a god. It was only after he was resurrected by *Isis* that he became a deity. He is the one who tamed the Egyptians and led them out of the barbarity of the Pre-Dynastic period when they were just primitive cannibals, battling with one another and obsessed with killing. *Osiris* taught the Egyptians agriculture and the precepts of leading a moral life. *Osiris* is pictured as a bull or as a glorified Pharaoh with the crown of Upper and Lower Egypt and carries a crook and a flail. On occasion, he is shown as a phoenix that arises from its ashes or a hawk. Sometimes the color of his skin in the frescoes has held its original hue, that of green. Green in the color of renewed life as in rebirth. On occasion, the skin is black, like that of humus, or very fertile earth.

※

NEBT-HET or NEPHTHYS

Nebt-het, the third daughter of *Nut* and *Geb* is a female warrior in the sense of a defender. She protects the temple and the religion from those who would assail it. She was spoken of as a warrior because she is also the protector during the pain of childbirth and the pain of the dying. *Nebt-het* is she who protects the mummy of the departed from marauders and those who violate the tombs. In addition, it is she who assists in the embalming process. She guards the canopic jars in the pyramids and tombs. Canopic jars are stone jars that hold the organs of the deceased. They are returned to the individual's remains, once the person receives their glorified body after they made their trip, also called *"Duat"* from the earthly world into the heaven world.

⚜

Nebt-het is a midwife who also aids Isis in the nursing of *Horus,* and is associated with those women throughout the ages who aided mothers in childbirth and provide milk for their children when necessary.

⚜

Her symbols are sometimes the wings of a falcon (for carrying the soul after death).

⚜

"Nephthys" is the Greek name of *Nebt-het.*

⚜

HORUS THE ELDER AND HORUS: THE DIVINE BABE

⚜

Horus the Elder was another son of *Nut* and *Geb.* He is portrayed as a human with a falcon head. He is seen as the protector of Kings. He was appointed to be the god of Lower Egypt, or the rich delta region at the mouth of the great Nile. Those were the most fertile and active areas of Egypt that was home to trade and subsequent wealth. His right eye represents the morning star or the sun, and the other eye is the moon. Every pharaoh is a deity and upon ascending to the throne has a "**Horus name**." The Pharaoh is the deity *Horus* in the flesh. He is god made man.

☙❧

Horus is the protagonist of all conflicts. After *Set* killed *Osiris,* as seen in the legend at the beginning of this Chapter, the conflict between *Horus* and *Set* started and continued for eighty years. The Egyptians called these battles "**Contend-ings**." In all their contendings, *Horus* always wins. It was said in the Pyramid texts that *Horus* and *Set* argued frequently over the dominion of Lower Egypt. *Set* wasn't content with Upper Egypt, as it was mostly a desert territory. In one of their battles, *Set* gouged out the left eye of *Horus* that stood for the moon. When the moon goes through its phases, it was said that it symbolizes the loss of eye in that fight. The story is "**told**" and "**retold**" monthly as the moon settles into its new moon phase, when it cannot be seen.

☙❧

In another fight, *Horus* is said to have cut off one of *Set's* testicles. That is demonstrated geo-physically by the infertility of the desert, the domain of *Set.*

☙❧

SET or SETH

Set is "**Bad Boy**" of the divine family. He married his sister, *Nebt-het.* He did, however, have redeeming qualities. He was a protector and a loving husband. He is a reconciled foe, but one who can nevermore be trusted, having lost the benefit of the doubt.

14

✦

Set was appointed the Lord of Upper Egypt, but was jealous of *Horus* and that was the heart of their conflicts. *Set* was manipulative and extremely devious. In the myth having to do with the murder of *Osiris,* he tricked *Osiris* into climbing into a large coffer. When *Osiris* did that, *Set* and his fellow conspirators slammed the lid closed, depriving him of breath.

✦

From the above story, comes one of the most important ceremonials performed on a deceased pharaoh – the opening of the mouth which will be explained later.

✦

Many of the *Set* myths have sexual themes, including homosexuality. Rape and sadomasochistic sexual were sometimes used in story contexts.

✦

Set is portrayed as a man with the head of a jackal. Other hieroglyphic representations are pigs and donkeys, for which the associations are obvious. He is patron of catastrophic storms and the parched desert.

✦

As a human, *Set* had red hair and the color red is associated with him. *Set* is also called the "***Cackler***." That's how the Egyptians characterized the barking of jackals.

At the end of the stories, it is said that *Set* was tried in the court of the gods, and then deprived of the dominion of both Lower and Upper Egypt. Historians have said that may have symbolized the union of the two halves of Egypt into one vast empire.

THOTH and ANUBIS

Thoth is often portrayed in the frescoes adorning the chambers inside the pyramids and temples. His most common depiction was of a man with the head of an ibis. He is associated with arbitration, having resolved disputes and he judges the good or evil of a man. He is also considered a master of writing, literature, wisdom and the sciences. On occasion, he is shown with the head of a baboon or with the pharaoh crown of the two kingdoms of Upper and Lower Egypt.

Anubis is the jackal-headed god of the afterlife. It was his role to **"*weigh the heart*"** in terms of good or evil to determine if a man deserves to be reborn to the magnificent world of the afterlife. He is the protector of the tombs and an embalmer. He is the guide for souls in the journey through the underworld, and into the afterlife. Sometimes he is pictured with the head of a wolf.

SOCIAL STRUCTURE

THE PHARAOH

☙❧

The pharaoh was the ruler of Egypt. When acting as ruler of Lower Egypt, he wore the red crown, the *"**Deshret**."* As ruler of Upper Egypt, he wore the white crown, the *"**Hadjet**."* When the two kingdoms were united, he wore a composite crown of red and white called the *Pschent*. Sometimes he simply wore a headdress called the *Nemes*. He presided at the highest of sacred feasts.

☙❧

As pharaoh, he was responsible to his people for peace and defense. It was his sworn duty to maintain *"**Maat**,"* or justice.

THE VIZIER

❧

The vizier was the first in command under the pharaoh. Although some have said the vizier lived a life of luxury, he was a busy man. Viziers were administrative, but had been known to have an artistic flair. It was they who organized for the residences, the zoning and the building of houses for the people. Extra attention was paid to the artisans, craftsmen and construction workers for the pyramids and the temples. They employed others to help organize the periodic festivals. Water resources had to be tended to and granaries had to be cared for. The vizier hired people to distribute from those granaries at times of shortage.

THE CHIEF TREASURER

❧

He was the "**tax collector**." Taxes weren't paid by coin or paper currency. They were paid in the form of goods like textiles, grain, silver or animals. Goods that weren't consumed by the officials were stored for the future needs of the country.

THE GENERAL

❧

Tribes of wandering nomads were replete. Sometimes they

raided the wealth and goods of Egypt. When treaties could not be drawn up, military forces had to be assembled.

THE PRIESTS

❧⚜❧

A priest presided at the sacred ceremonies, particularly with regard to the embalming of the Pharaoh's body. He had a tremendous obligation to be sure that all the prescriptions of the pharaoh and of their sacred texts were followed. If he failed, the offense was punishable by death.

THE SCRIBES

He was the official in charge of record-keeping, especially including the telling of the stories of the gods. These were recited to the people in the temple. He also supervised the hieroglyphic texts that related the life of the pharaoh and were preserved on the chamber walls inside the pyramids.

THE GREAT PYRAMID OF KHUFU
AKA CHEOPS 2589-2566 BC

৩৯৫

Every pharaoh was given a "***Horus name***." The *Horus* name is represented as a bas-relief called a "***serekh***." It is an oblong tablet inside of which is the shape of the outer walls of a building. Inside that, there is another oblong carving of buildings or the like that represents the city or town in which the pharaoh was born. On top of the inner oblong there is a falcon on top, representing *Horus*. That is how the pharaoh is to be addressed once he had ascended to the throne. In Khufu's case, his *Horus* name was *Mejedu*. It means "***Horus who strikes***."

৩৯৫

According to the ancient historian, Herodotus, Khufu

> *"plunged into all manner of wickedness. He closed the*
> *temples, and forbade the Egyptians to offer*
> *sacrifice."*

Although many historians categorized him as anti-religious, he wasn't. He asked his son to tell him tales of the gods, and many of those have been recorded on papyri. One of the reasons for his refusal to permit his people to worship was to keep the secrets of the afterlife and resurrection to himself. Some later historians indicate that Khufu repented of that, and again permitted his people to worship at the public temples.

৩৩

Khufu was obsessed with immortality. He hired over 97 mortuary priests to prepare him for a luxurious after-life. Because he wished to achieve eternal fame, he had builders plan on a huge and grand pyramid in which to spend his days as he came and went to the heaven-world. Egyptians believed that the "*ka*," the soul, returned to the body as it made trips to and from heaven.

৩৩

Khufu did achieve the fame he craved, as his is the largest pyramid at Giza. The pyramid lies alongside a former harbor at the Wadi al-Jarf. A "*wadi*" is a valley created by the bed of a waterway that is only filled with water when the Nile floods.

৩৩

There was full-time employment available when Khufu started the construction of his pyramid. Toward the building effort, Khufu hired 20,000 men, divided and subdivided into work gangs and according to their skills. Khufu increased the number of workers when the Nile flooded because the farms couldn't be worked until the water subsided. The excess water was also extremely useful because the huge limestone blocks could be transported on barges pulled by donkeys and men. The external faces of the pyramid were coated with polished marble, but the marble was robbed over the centuries. Hence, a jagged appearance is what is seen in photographs.

◊≫◊

The weight of these stones was a much as 31 tons. The height of the enormous structure is about 490' high. Estimates projected indicate that it took about 30 years to build!

◊≫◊

The chamber in which the sarcophagus is placed was at the approximate center of the pyramid. There is a number of corridors that thread through the artifice. The entrance is on the North face, and descends into a downward fork. One of the corridors from the entrance leads to a false burial chamber that lies under the pyramid. The other descending corridor leads to an ascending hallway and opens into the "*Grand Gallery*." At the bottom of the Grand Gallery, there is a horizontal corridor leading to the Queen's chamber.

◊≫◊

If one continues along the Grand Gallery, they observe painted frescoes on the walls telling the story of the King's life along with the gods as companions. Following the Grand Gallery is the King's Chamber. The King's Chamber is at the base of a five-story structure.

◊≫◊

From the King's Chamber, there was an air vent, used not only for air, but to allow the King to come and go to the heaven-world at will. There was also another air vent from the end of the Great Gallery. The architects of the pyramid were skilled in physics, geometry and the earth sciences. The interior temperature of the pyramid is a steady 68° F!

❧✷❧

In the tomb chamber, the archeologists discovered a canopy bed, a carrying chair of ebony, two sitting chairs, copper tools, alabaster jars, gold knives, a copper basin and a golden manicure set. The alabaster pots were inlaid with semi-precious jewels.

❧✷❧

The entire process of building the pyramid for Khufu plunged the country into debt. Because of some fortunately fruitful harvests, the Egyptians were able to recover, but never recovered the wealth it enjoyed during Khufu's reign.

THE MORBID EMBALMING
PROCESS

৩৫৩

The body was first washed in palm wine and water. Then the embalmers cut open the left side of the body and remove the major organs, except for the heart. These organs are stored in "*canopic*" jars packed with natron, a mineral salt. There were four jars used:

৩৫৩

A Falcon-headed jar for the intestines
A Human-headed jar for the liver
A Jackal-headed jar for the stomach
A Baboon-headed jar for the lungs

৩৫৩

Because the heart was considered to be the seat of intelligence and emotion, it was left inside the body.

※

The brain was removed through a grisly but delicate process. A long metal hook is inserted through one of the nostrils, then worked up through the nasal passages and upwards until it hits the brain. Little by little the brain is removed and burned. The Egyptians knew nothing about the vital function that the brain serves.

※

The viscera is then packed with natron salt, and the body is completely covered with the salt. The natron dries out the inside of the body. After forty days, the embalmers return, remove the salt and rewash the body. Then the hollow area inside the body is stuffed with linens, sawdust or leaves.

OPENING OF THE MOUTH

❧

I t was feared that, if a pharaoh couldn't open his mouth, he wouldn't be able breath, speak or eat. Initially, it was thought that this was performed symbolically via texts on papyri. However, recently there has been some anatomical evidence found that a physical procedure was performed. The mouth was gently forced open with forceps, and the interior of the mouth was washed out. Generally, the mouth wasn't opened widely, just sufficient enough to allow for speech.

❧

While this is being done, a funerary priest recites the sacred words:

❧

"Hail god, Tem (Ra, the setting sun), grant me the

sweet breath that dwells in your nostrils. I embrace the throne...and I keep watch over the egg of the great Cackler (Set). I germinate as it germinates; I live as it lives, and my breath is its breath."

THE WRAPPING OF THE MUMMY

❧

A t the end, the outside of the body is washed with oil, most likely olive oil, to return moisture and elasticity to it, because the natron had dried up the skin. The body is wrapped in strips of linen, and amulets are placed on top of each level of wrapping.

❧

The embalmers, the scribe and the priest then re-read the instructions carefully to see that this was done properly according to the instructions in their sacred book:

❧

> *"...after he has been cleansed and purified, and when he is arrayed in apparel, and is shod with white leather sandals, and his eyes have been painted with antimony, and his body has been anointed*

with unguent, and when he has made offerings of oxen, and birds, and incense, and cakes and ale and garden herbs, you shall write a chapter and (then) the deceased shall flourish and his children shall flourish and his name shall never fall into oblivion...and he will follow Osiris always and forever."

❧ III ❧
THE COMING OF THE HYKSOS

❦

The Old Kingdom under Khufu was wealthy, but he and succeeding pharaohs had spent much of country's treasury on their pyramids. In addition, centuries bring with them cycles of plenty and famine. Not only that, but the mere fact that populations increase exponentially during times of prosperity places a burden upon future generations. The wealth of the pharaohs often blinded them to the cry of human need, and the obsession with the fact that the nature of their afterlife depended solely upon their preparations contributed to the enormous expense. In addition, he and his successors made generous gifts of land and money to the priests and aristocrats of the time.

❦

Toward the end of the Old Kingdom, Khufu's successors had more limited resources, and the period of huge pyramid building had to cease. Although the hereditary line of the pharaohs continued, it was the priesthood who held all the power. Egypt was split into "nomarchies" ruled by kings or "nomarchs." These were smaller territories. From time to time, border conflicts erupted as each king became envious of the property of other kingdoms in the vicinity.

⚜

During the Old Kingdom, Memphis, located just South of the Nile delta, was its capital. The ambitious kings waged seasonal wars and went on foreign campaigns to conquer more territory. Desirous of expanding Southward, they constantly assaulted Nubia. Nubia is what is known as Northern Sudan today. Because the bulk of the military forces under the nomarchs moved Southward, the capital was moved from Memphis in the Delta region to Herakleopolis, which was more centrally located.

THE DANCES OF THE DANGA
DWARFS

৩%৯

When the Egyptians penetrated further South into Nubia and beyond, the explorers preceded them. In Africa around the area of present-day Tanzania, they captured and brought back "***Danga Dwarfs***" who could perform the dances of the gods. Much of that information was recorded on cuneiform tablets from the Assyrians who may have likewise captured the Danga dwarfs also. There is confusion as to whether or not these were humans afflicted with dwarfism or small apes. Given the information about the origin of the Danga dwarfs, that is, Tanzania and areas north of the Congo River, they were most likely chimpanzees. Chimps are terrific imitators and most likely learned to perform those dances from the explorers and priests. Egyptian frescoes sometimes pictured Thoth - the god of literature - accompanied by Danga dwarfs.

৩%৯

The Pharaoh at that time was Pepi II (circa 2184 BC) and he was delighted with the Dangas whom he kept with him in his courtyards.

Pepi II, it is said, ruled for 90 years which is highly unusual for primitive man without the benefit of modern medicine. He was an old man who quite understandably lacked the ambition of youth and grew progressively uninterested in administering the various normarchs in Egypt.

THE NEW INVADER

❦

The greedy priesthood and nomarchs of Egypt clamored for more land grants and gifts from the pharaoh's treasury and the weary pharaoh gave in to them. Popular discontent arose as the other nobles and the commoners watched helplessly as their lands were being seized.

❦

As noted earlier, the capital had been moved Southward to Herakleopolis. That meant that less attention was directed toward management of the Delta region. Due to that, it was invaded by Bedouin tribal nomads from the Maghreb (North Africa). It may have also been assaulted by what was called the "*Sea People*." Their identity by the old historians is unknown, so they may have been from Southern Europe or migrants from Asia that built ships and sailed the Mediterranean.

Egypt was split in the Delta region (Lower Egypt) and territories South of there (Upper Egypt) was now expanding Southward toward Thebes. All of the regions were in constant conflict and anarchy prevailed.

ADMONITIONS OF A SAGE

❧

The sage at Herakleopolis described the devastation and horrors that prevailed and effectively shut the curtain on the Old Kingdom, just as the Middle Kingdom was struggling to be borne. The dying breath of the old regime was wretched and miserable. The sage said:

❧

"Magical spells are divulged...Butchers transgress with geese who are given to the gods instead of oxen...The land is left over to its weariness like the cutting of flax. Noise is not lacking in years of noise. There is no end to noise..."

❧

"Mirth has perished, and is no longer made. It is groaning that fills the land, mingled with

lamentations. All animals, their hearts weep. Cattle moan because of the state of the land. The virtuous man walks in mourning because of what has happened in the land. Great and small say: 'I wish I might die.' Little children say: 'My mother ought never have given birth to me.' Men throw themselves in the river to be devoured by crocodiles. The fate of the dead is not much better than that of the living. Many dead men are buried in the river. The stream is a sepulcher and the place of entombment has become a stream."

MENTUHOTEP II 2065-2060 BC &
THE BLACK KINGS

৬১৯১

From Thebeswhere the famous mortuary sites of Karnak and Luxor are situated, came Mentuhotep. The Egyptians were most fortunate, as this noted Pharaoh was blessed with military and administrative abilities surpassing that of prior pharaohs. He gave rise to what is sometimes classified as the 11th Dynasty. He quelled the rebellious populations around Herakleopolis and even North of there all the way to the Delta. Much of his wisdom is reflected in the fact that he preferred making treaties to warfare and tried to avoid the bloody alternative which had subjected Egypt to barrenness and poverty. In terms of the Maghreb tribesmen who now settled in Lower Egypt, the truce was a precarious one, and Memtuhotep had to pacify them regularly with gifts and re-establishment of the devastated farmlands.

৬১৯১

In Nubia, he had to assert his authority and dispatched some major military campaigns. To do so, he confiscated their ill-gotten lands of the nomads – lands which he had conquered from poor commoners and other nomarchs. By that time, the Kings of these smaller nomarchs had transformed their rule to be hereditary. Mentuhotep II passed a ban on that practice, and wars of succession practically disappeared. Mentuhotep's successor and son, Mentuhotep III followed in the footsteps of his father. He established a court system. All people, regardless of whether they were nobles or commoners were considered equal in the eyes of the law – a truly revolutionary concept for the time.

࿇

He then reunited Lower Egypt with that of Upper Egypt. The capital was now moved to Thebes. The reunification of the two kingdoms of Egypt was his most notable accomplishment.

ECONOMICAL AND RELIGIOUS
IMPROVEMENTS

༺✿༻

Because of the anarchical situation that dominated Egypt during the civil wars, the Nile was out of control. During better times, irrigation ditches were dug from the Nile to keep the farmlands moist during the growing season. The trenches were in a state of total dysfunction. Mentuhotep improved the irrigation channels and had them rebuilt.

༺✿༻

The temples and shrines had been destroyed during the great wars, and Mentuhotep reconstructed them.

༺✿༻

In terms of religion, Mentuhotep began a series of reforms by restoring interest in *Amon-Ra* as the chief god. That effort continued into the New Kingdom.

❧❦❧

During his reign, Mentuhotep indicated that everyone – not just the pharaohs and nobles – had the right to be judged by *Osiris* after death. That began a period in which individual tombs for the architects and craftsmen could be built. It ushered in a sense of respect for the lives and deaths of all people.

MORTUARY TEMPLE OF
MENTUHOTEP

❦

Mentuhotep's temple lies on the Nile shores across from the Temple of Karnak, famed for its archeological value as well. It is a temple complex that houses the tombs of his predecessors and successors too. It's located at the cliff town of Deir al-Bahri in the famous Valley of the Kings.

❦

Although the temple was ornate and quite admirable when it was newly built, it did not require the enormous expense of the great pyramids. Mentuhotep was a more frugal man, and realized that all a country's wealth should not be spent in such a wasteful manner.

❦

Mentuhotep's temple had many colonnades of intricately

carved pillars. A magnificent courtyard was planted with flower beds, sycamore and tamarisk trees. An elaborate irrigation system was installed and maintained by a temple staff. There was a causeway that led to an upper-story temple, also containing a colonnade. Within the complex was a tomb for one of his wives.

⚜

Reliefs show carvings of Mentuhotep II along with the deities *Neb-het, Set, Horus* and others. Mentuhotep felt that the kings and pharaohs must merit the divinity status and maintain it. In an inscription above the deity relief it states:

⚜

> *"In the Old Kingdom, the king had been the lord of the pyramid complex. Now he is reduced to a human ruler dependent on the gods' good will. His immortality is no longer innate; it has to be bestowed on him by the gods."*

⚜

The tomb of Mentuhotep was excessively plundered by grave robbers. However, one of the most interesting artifacts that remained was that of a stone model of a granary, used to store grain for the people during the dry seasons. There is an entrance in the model and carefully carved figures of busy workers carrying in the grain and pouring it into giant bins that were protected from moisture and inclement weather.

⚜

There were also models of ships and bakeries serving as demonstrations of the kinds of occupations in which the Egyptians engaged. Offerings to the gods were also found in the excavations including a scepter, cattle skulls, and bowls containing remnants of barley, fruits and bread. And – by the way – the Ancient Egyptians made beer! It was their favorite beverage.

AMENEMHAT III 1850-1800 BC

❧

A menemhat III was one of the most brilliant and courageous pharaohs that ruled the two kingdoms of Egypt. He continued the policy that his father established abolishing the power of the nomarchs. During the initial period of the Middle Kingdom, these nomarchs had even become more powerful than the pharaohs themselves and continually instigated wars between the small city-states. It was during this period that Nubia separated itself from the rest of Egypt.

❧

Like Mentuhotep, Amenemhat III continued the irrigation projects. During his reign it was said that the desert *"blossomed like the rose."*

❧

Unfortunately, the disintegration that occurred following his reign remain shrouded in mystery. Quite possibly, it could have been caused by a succession of weaker kings and queens. In addition, famines tended to occur regularly in Egypt.

INVASION OF THE "SHEPHERD KINGS"

৩২৩

Manetho, a priest in the 3rd Century BC, wrote the history of Egypt. As a man who lived at time close to that of the pharaohs themselves, he reflects the tenor and attitudes of the Egyptians in this work. When he discussed the Middle Kingdom, he spoke of a calamitous event:

৩২৩

"God was displeased with us and there came up
unexpectedly from the East men of an ignoble race
who had the audacity to invade our land."

৩২৩

They were the Hittites, also called the "**Hyksos**" in older texts. Hittites are associated with various regions throughout the Bronze Age (circa 2300 BC- 1200 BC) The term

"**Hittite**" is most commonly associated with Anatolia (Turkey). However, during this era it was an empire that extended from Eastern Anatolia, the coast of the Levant and the Delta regions of Egypt. Artifacts of Hyksos-Egyptian origin are housed in Turkey. The tribes that invaded Egypt appeared to have been warlike Syro-Palestinian nomads and had a marked Semitic facial appearance, as can be seen in the statuettes. The term "**Shepherd Kings**" appears to be a misnomer and scholars have suggested that it may have been an improper translation of Manetho's histories.

࿓

The ancient historian, Josephus, reported that the Hyksos were able to take over the Delta in Lower Egypt without a fight. The Hyksos forces were massive – as many as 30,000 men. Their armies were composed of infantrymen and charioteers. One can easily see how such as massive force could have subdued the Delta regions of Egypt.

THE CHARIOT

❧

The chariot was constructed of wood and covered with bronze or leather. A single spoke ran through it supporting the wheels. To the chariot, a sturdy horse was yoked. These chariots were amazingly swift and maneuverable.

❧

The most frequently used weapon was a slashing sword shaped like a sickle, but with its sharp blade on the outside. Another common weapon was a heavy axe. Spears were popular as were bows and arrows. Later on, they developed very vicious-looking daggers and longer stabbing swords.

SALITIS – THE FIRST HYKSOS KING (1650-1620 BC)

❦

S alitis was equivalent to a sultan. About him, Manetho said:

❦

*"After they invaded, they made one of their number,
whose name was Salitiis, king. He resided in
Memphis and exacted tribute from both the upper
and lower country, leaving fortresses in the most
strategic places...He made the city of Avaris on
the East Bank of the Nile."*

❦

Avaris is on the Eastern edge of the Nile Delta. It lies very close to the Sinai Peninsula.

❦

The Hyksos or Hittite kings sometimes permit the pharaonic line to continue, but the Hittite kings had the real power in the territory.

ABRAHAM AKA IBRAHIM OF UR

ॐ

Abraham aka Ibrahim enters the history texts during the reign of Salitis. His story is told not only in the Bible, but in the cuneiform tablets in Mesopotamia and the papyrus of Turin. It is said that he left Ur in Mesopotamia and migrated South West. He and his family had gone into the Delta area and settled among the people there prior to the arrival of the Hittites. He was a shepherd. In the Christian bible, this land was referred to as "***Goshen***." In the Hebrew scriptures, called the *Tanakh,* the Hittites were called the "***Horites***." After the Hittite invasion, the Hebrews were put into slavery.

THE HIPPOPOTAMUS POOL AND
THE HORRIBLE MUMMY

❧

Seqenenre Tao was the pharaoh from 1560 BC. His death date is unknown. Early in his reign, the very powerful Hittite king, Apepi, sent a missive to Seqenenre complaining about the hippotamuses he was raising in a giant pool. Apparently they were extremely noisy and Apepi claimed he could hear them when he was trying to go to sleep.

❧

They exchanged messages full of contempt and peppered with threats. As result of the highly-charged dialogue, they faced one another at Thebes. In the 19th Century the mummy of Seqenenre was found in the Valley of the Kings and unwrapped. A foul smell arose as the unwrapping was in process, revealing that normal mummification procedure of adding the natron salts had been skipped. The internal organs also weren't removed. The skull had extremely vicious gashes, holes and cracks. According to the historian, Maspero:

ಠಠ

"A blow from an axe must have severed part of his left cheek, exposed the teeth, fractured the jaw, and sent him senseless to the ground; another blow must have seriously injured the skull, and a dagger or javelin has cut open the forehead on the right side, a little above the eye. His body must have remained lying where it fell for some time: when found, decomposition had set in, and embalming had to be hastily performed as best it might."

ಠಠ

His is the most poorly preserved mummy ever found in Egypt. No wonder no tomb robber ever purloined it!

JOSEPH, DESCENDANT OF ABRAHAM, AND KING APEPI

☙❧

I t was during the reign of the Hittite King, Apepi, that the Hebrew Joseph was banished by his brothers and arrived in Egypt. Because of his skills in reading dreams, he assisted Apepi in avoiding a famine and became a prime minister under him.

THE SLEEPY ERA OF THE
HITTITE KINGS

❦

The Hittite kings were many and most of them were but petty and opportunistic nomarchs. The Egyptians, in the meantime, continued to maintain and improve their irrigation systems, and continued to pacify the Kings with their tributes. Many of these kings moreover were more interested in the events of Asia Minor and let the hardworking Egyptians manage on their own. This worked well for the Egyptians, as they kept refurbishing their treasuries.

❦

The Hittites were nevertheless intensely disliked, and the Egyptians awaited the coming of a new pharaoh who would rescue them from these little dictatorships. In the Late Kingdom it happened.

ATHMOSIS: THE PHARAOH WHO
REUNITED EGYPT (1549-1524 BC)

※

U nder the Pharaoh Athmosis aka Athmose, the first task was to go back to the wayward Nubia which had seceded from Egypt during the reign of Amenumhat III (see prior Chapter). He had been ruling from Thebes, so took his army Southward as far as the Second Cataract. The "*cataracts*" were areas where there were rapids in the Nile. He easily reconquered Nubia, as they had been caught unaware.

※

Athmosis decided to drive out the Hittites altogether. They had grown fat and lazy and the conquest was actually much easier than some histories suggest. First, he conquered many of the city-states in the Delta, and then turned back and targeted the Hittite capital of Avaris. It was a relatively matter, as the minor kings of the Southern coastal regions were split up into small communities and spent their time warring with each other. Their interests lay only in power, so they ignored the economic needs of the common people. The people there cared very little about the petty bickering of the royal families and their military, so were very much in favor of Athmosis' forces.

⚙

After the Hittites retreated from Avaris, they fled to Gaza.

⚙

Athmosis then gave chase. After crossing the Northern Sinai Peninsula, he moved toward the town of Sharuhen. Sharuhen is now called Tell al-Farah South and lies in the Negev desert. Athmosis wanted the Hittites to retreat even further North so as not to be able to enter Egypt as easily as they had done before. Once he reached Sharuhen, he put the town under a siege. There were barely any survivors when he left there.

⚙

Athmosis married his sister, also of royal descent, who co-ruled with him as Queen Athmose Nefertari. She should not be confused with Queen Nefertari, the wife of Rameses II who lived much later.

⚙

Nefertari was greatly loved by the people, especially for putting vigor into the temple feasts and religious practices of *Amon-Ra*. Queen Athmose Nefertari was described as being an intelligent sovereign quite capable of ruling the country in her husband's absences while he was out on military campaigns. From the statues that were found in archeological sites, Nefertari was a poised and beautiful Black woman.

⚜

The Queen maintained the Egyptian administration in Thebes, and she ruled as Pharaoh after Athmosis died.

THE EXHUMATION AND
REBURIAL

❧

A thmosis did have a pyramid built for himself. It was
West of Thebes on the Nile. Due to excessive
flooding from the Nile, it was partially destroyed in
later years.

❧

Grave robbers were very common in Ancient Egypt, and it
became a regular practice to safeguard the Pharaoh's body by
exhuming the body and burying it elsewhere. Most historians
believe that happened in Athmosis' case. Sometimes, memo-
rials are erected in the place of tombs to trick grave robbers
into thinking that there are mummies and treasures below.

❧

In the 19ᵗʰ Century, Athmosis' actual mummy was discovered
in the Valley of the Kings. When it was examined by the

archeologists, there was definite evidence that his body had been violated after he was buried because his head was removed from the body and his nose was smashed. When they examined the body, the archeologists noted that he showed the presence of prominent front teeth, a hereditary trait of the royal family.

THE MEMORIAL OF ATHMOSIS

❀

I n the Valley of the Kings, Athmosis is memorialized for
having reunited Egypt. An excerpt from his epitaph:

❀

"*Golden Horus (the pharaoh), great of forms, born in
beauty, Golden Horus who knotted together the
two lands, King of Upper and Lower Egypt...may
he live (be resurrected) prosper and be healthy –
who has reduced to obedience the two lands, great
of awe, mighty in apparition as those who bow
down, their gods bring him life and fortune,
whose brilliance creates the light...and he makes
his chapel known.*"

THE ACCOMPLISHED PHARAOH QUEEN HATSHEPSUT (CIRCA 1507-1479 BC)

৩৯৯

She was married to Thutmosis II, but served as pharaoh after he died. His brother, Thutmosis III was too young to assume the position of pharaoh.

৩৯৯

During her reign, Hatshepsut set out on a building campaign in Egypt that could rival that of Caesar Augustus of Ancient Rome. In addition, he opened up many new trade routes that boosted the economic success of all the Egyptians.

BUILDINGS

꧁❀꧂

Temples and places of worship meant far more to the Egyptians than churches do today. They were gathering places and beautiful buildings in which the Egyptians could come and offer sacrifice and prayers. Religion was a means of bonding and unity.

꧁❀꧂

Many of the temple sites had been desecrated by the Hittite rulers, and Hatshepsut felt it would boost morale by showing the Egyptians that the cruel oppression was over. In addition, these projects served as a means of steady employment for the construction workers, furniture manufacturers, artisans, scribes, maintenance personnel and priests. During her reign she had constructed many buildings among which are:

꧁❀꧂

- the precinct of Mut, a garden, pool and temple dedicated to the deity Mut

- monuments at the Temple of Karnak

- the "***Red Chapel***" with bronze plates, statuary and carvings

- two obelisks

- the Temple of Pakhet, a minor goddess portrayed as a lioness, who controls the Nile floods

- The Djeser-Djeset, of "***Sublime of Sublimes***" which is a magnificent three-story colonnaded temple with many gardens and terraces. This was also to be her mortuary temple and is visited by tourists.

- the "***Speos Artemidos***," which is an underground temple carved into the base of a cliff.

Hatshepsut has a heartfelt and loving inscription on the Speos Artemidos telling her people and future generations what she has tried to do to restore Egypt after the heartless destruction wrought by the Hittites. It reads:

"Hear ye, all people and folk as many as they may be,
I have done these things through the counsel of

my heart. I have not slept forgetfully, but I have restored that which had been ruined. I have raised up that which has gone to pieces formerly, since the Asiatics were in the midst of Avaris of the Northland, and vagabonds were in the midst of them, overthrowing that which has been made."

❦

All of these temples had beautiful statues, carvings and decorations within. It is reported that every major museum had one or more of Hatshepsut's statues and artifacts in their collections.

VANDALISM BY FUTURE PHARAOHS!

❦

Many of the pharaohs from future regimes attempted to lay claim to some of these beautiful structures. Many even had Queen Hatshepsut's name scratched out and their own cartouche (hieroglyphic name plate) put in its place! One of the most noted of the Late Kingdom pharaohs, Seti I, was identified by archeologists as being guilty of purloining some of Hatshepsut's treasures. Evidence also indicated that he tried to insert his name inside the Speos Artemidos Temple.

❦

This vandalism became extreme in time, as jealous male pharaohs attempted to remove her name from the historical records altogether. However, some clever artisans carved her name in otherwise hidden places so that Egyptologists could uncover the mystery. Despite that, to this day archeologists and historians still argue about the artifacts and accomplishments of her regime as told in the ancient hieroglyphics.

ECONOMIC BOON

෯෧ඁ

Queen Hashepsut re-established the devastated system for accessing the Land of Put. The identity of Put is contested, but it's agreed by most to be in Northern Somalia It had a major port and city accessible to all the traders and caravans in Eastern Africa, the Western Arabian Peninsula, and even Canaan (Jordan, Israel and Palestine). Thousands of products, minerals, spices, wine, cloth, ivory, gold, silver, wild animals, trees, plants and many other products were brought to its shores. This merchant traffic brought wealth to Egypt and the people flourished under good Queen Hatshepsut.

HATSHEPSUT AND MOSES

✦

A lthough there is a lot of disagreement among Biblical and historical scholars as to who was the pharaoh during the Exodus, a great many of them agree that Hatshepsut was the pharaoh's daughter who cared for Moses as an infant. The pharaoh was Thutmosis I. Hatshepsut married his son, Thutmosis II, but he died shortly thereafter. In the Christian Bible, it is said that she wanted to adopt Moses officially and asked him to take over as pharaoh, but he refused. In the book of the Hebrews, Chapter 11, verse 24, it says:

✦

"By faith Moses, when he had grown up, refused to be known as the son of the pharaoh's daughter."

✦

That meant, in essence, that he could have been the next pharaoh because of the adoption. Moses also refused because he felt it was his mission to lead the Israelites out of Egypt. They had been taken into slavery when the Hittites were in control.

HATSHEPSUT DIES

❦

The noted Egyptologist, Zahi Hawass, head of Egypt's Department of Antiquities for many years, discovered the location of her remains. Due to clinical analysis, it was concluded that she died from bone cancer, a very painful kind of cancer. One of the theories about a contributing factor was the use of a carcinogenic skin cream, although that couldn't be the main cause.

❦

As indicated earlier, sometimes future pharaohs remove the hieroglyphic mentions of a predecessor's name. Another theory stems from the fact that it was incredibly expensive to build an elaborate tomb to oneself, so it may have been made of segments from older tombs and structures.

❦ IV ❧

THUTMOSIS III
(1479-1425 BC)

✥

The Pharaoh Queen Hatshepsut (see Chapter 2) was the step-mother of Thutmosis III. He was the son of her husband's concubine, Iset. Hatshepsut was co-regent because Thutmosis was too young to assume the role. In essence, she was the "Queen Mother."

✥

It was time for revenge against the Hittites. They occupied the lands of Canaan, and this was a chance for the Egyptians to expand their empire. He proceeded with his armies across the Sinai Peninsula and headed North Ward toward the Levant. The Levant is current day Gaza, Israel, Lebanon and Western Syria. His navy was well-developed under the regime of his mother Hatshepsut, so he utilized it efficiently. From the Hittites who occupied Egypt for so many years, he learned about the uses of the chariots and had ones built for his own military forces.

THE BATTLE OF MEGIDDO
1457 BC

࿄

I n Canaan, the Hittites and the indigent population of
Canaan defended themselves. At the crucial city of
Megiddo, they had three routes to follow, but took the
Northern route. The defenders under the king of Kadesh
moved South to challenge them. (Kadesh is located on the
Southern border of Syria.) When the armies of Kadesh
reached Megiddo, they unwisely collected themselves at the
city gates. Thutmosis split his army into three divisions.
Before they assailed the city gates, the Hittites looted the
Canaanite camps. First they assaulted the foot soldiers and
then pursued the hidden charioteers of Thutmosis because
they knew where they were. When the Canaanites retreated
behind the city walls of Megiddo, Thutmosis and his men
sieged it until the occupiers were forced to surrender. On one
of the stelae describing Thutmosis' battle, it says:

࿄

"*There was no end to men and horses. When they (Thutmosis men) came, their hearts were courageous and no fear was in their hearts. The powerful one cast them down. He was strong of arm, trampling down his enemies. He is the king who fights alone, no throng is surrounding his heart. He is more courageous than the millions in the great army, one does not find his like, a warrior, courageous on the battlefield, one cannot resist him...He flashes like a star crossing the sky.*"

ANNEXATION OF CANAAN

࿇

At the mortuary temple complex at Karnak, the archeologists discovered stone wall carvings telling of Thutmosis' annexations in Canaan. Canaan was at the heart of the territories of the Hittites. The hieroglyphic script relates how the city-states in Canaan paid tribute to Thutmosis and sent complaints and narrations about their local governmental activities. The delegates of Thutmosis were in charge of handling disputes and maintaining peace and order so that the people were able to engage in farming, fishing and mercantile trade.

SUBJUGATION OF SYRIA AND PHOENICIA

※

Thutmosis conducted many military campaigns throughout the Levant. On his fifth, sixth and seventh efforts there, he conquered the important port of Kadesh, a city along the great Orontes River leading out to the Eastern Mediterranean Sea. The current location of Kadesh can only be identified by ruins at Tell Nebi Mend, about 15 miles (24 KM) South West of the current city of Homs in Syria.

※

The Syrians were extremely rebellious and Thutmosis had to take extreme measures to subdue them. He kidnapped the children of nobles, and deprived the region of some of their grain so that they couldn't finance future rebellions. Future pharaohs also had a great deal of trouble quelling revolts there.

In Phoenicia (current-day Lebanon), he utilized the ports to obtain foodstuffs, grain, textiles and precious stones. The positive benefit to the Phoenicians was the fact that it stimulated local trade and wealth. The Phoenicians were famous for their naval skills and their shipbuilding industry.

HE KILLED SEVEN LIONS WITH ONE SHOT!

Thutmosis spent many years in the Levant and even more territory East of there in Mesopotamia. The hieroglyphic tablets found at Karnak tell tales of Thutmosis and his companions in fishing and hunting expeditions on the Euphrates River. Most fishermen exaggerate the size of their catch. Egyptian hunters were no exception, as can be seen in some of the engravings about the pharaoh:

> *"When he spent a moment of recreation hunting in*
> *any foreign land, the quantity that he captured*
> *was greater than what the entire army achieved.*
> *He slew seven lions by shooting in an instant. He*
> *captured a herd of twelve wild bulls in an hour."*

The scripts about the fishing expeditions of the Egyptians are numerous and read like manuals about the breeding habits of

the fish, their behavior, the kind of hooks to use and techniques for catching them.

MITANNIA

Mitannia was an area located between the Euphrates and Tigris River, in present-day Western Iran, Iraq and sections of Eastern Syria, including the important city of Aleppo. This was the target of Thutmosis' next military endeavor – an effort continued by his successor several generations later – Akhenaten.

Mitannia was an economically healthy area as it lay in the fertile region of two rivers. Mercantile trade flourished. Although they had the wealth to defend themselves these people were more interested in working than fighting. Thus they were easily annexed. Whenever they got word that the Egyptian pharaoh was in the area with his forces, the nobles hid in the caves until they left. That way, their lives were spared and they could return to exercise control over their respective areas.

There were very few Hittites in this area for two reasons:

- Most of Mitannia occupied a geographic area further East from the Hittites' seat of control

- The princes and kings of Mitannia were much more inclined to make treaties even with the conquering Egyptians, agreeing to pay tributes to them

۞

The cooperative relationship with Thutmosis III and his successors was to the mutual advantage of both Mittannia and Egypt. Mittannia and Egypt both wanted keep the Hittites away from the region, so armies from the two nations maintained defenses and fortifications. That forced the Hittites to retreat back to Anatolia where they were in prior centuries.

AKHENATEN (1353-1336 BC): HIS BLASPHEMY!

☙❧

O ften the pharaohs are identified by two names – their birth name and the name they assume upon their ascension to their thrones. Akhenaten's birth name was Amenhotep IV. Akhenaten did something that was considered scandalous in terms of the religious beliefs of the Ancient Egyptians.

☙❧

Early in his reign, Akhenaten rejected the traditional panthe- istic beliefs in favor of monotheism. He rejected *Amon* or *Amun* in favor of *"**Ra**,"* or *"**Aten**,"* and used the symbol of the sun to represent this one god. Many of the carvings show the sun with many rays that touch the people and objects on the earth to show that this one god is everywhere manifest.

☙❧

Below is an excerpt from the Hymn to Aten:

☾✺☽

> *"How manifold it is, what you have made!*
> *They are hidden from the face of man.*
> *O sole god, like whom there is no other!*
> *You created the world according to your desire,*
> *While you were alone: All men, cattle and wild*
>   *beasts,*
> *Whatever is on earth, going upon its feet,*
> *And what is on high, flying with its wings."*

☾✺☽

As for himself, Akhenaten used the term "**Prophet of Ra-Horakhte**," meaning "**Ra of the Horizon**." He also transferred the capitol to the city of Armana which he called "**Akhenaten**." He renamed the sole god "**Aten**."

☾✺☽

Furthermore, Akhenaton proclaimed himself the son of Aten and the one person who interceded with *Aten* on behalf of his people. People had stone carvings of their gods in their homes, but Akhenaten made them replace those with statues of *Aten,* portrayed as a disc like the sun.

☾✺☽

Thebes was the dwelling of all the Egyptian priests who promoted the worship of many deities. These priests were elitists who restricted public access to certain areas of the temple, reserving those chambers only for themselves.

He also closed down many of the temples to *Amun* and other deities. In addition, he wanted everyone to have access to his temples to *Aten*. He removed some of the stone carvings of other gods from many of the temples.

One of most peculiar facts that surfaced in excavations was the disappearance of male genitalia from statues of Akhenaten himself. He believed that *Aten* was neither male nor female, but androgynous, and that may have been an attempt to portray himself as a mother AND a father figure.

He also wanted to be sculpted realistically rather than as some glorified super-hero. Therefore, he and his wife were shown with protruding abdomens. Akhenaten himself had carvings of his head in such a way that his features matched those observed in his actual mummy. He had an elongated face with a sharply pointed chin, evidence of a cleft palate and delicate features.

There were some questions raised by archeologists indicating that Akhenaten had a wife before he married Nefertiti, the Queen noted for her beauty. It is possible that this woman was Akhenaten's own sister. Her name is as yet unknown, but he did have children by her, one of whom was Tutankhamun.

When the statuary showed Akhenaten with his wife, Nefertiti, there was no reluctance to show affection in order to demonstrate the love of a husband for his wife. In one statue, in particular, the royal couple is shown holding hands. This is unusual and never depicted in any other Egyptian sculptures. The beautiful Queen, Nefertiti, ruled alongside Akhenaten. There is little written in the ancient records about her life, but there are quite a number of sculptures and paintings of her in Ancient Egypt.

⚬⚬⚬

Usually the inscriptions and carvings of Ancient Egypt showed the pharaoh or a god as holding one *ankh,* which is the symbol of god granting the gift of the breath of life. In those representations of *Aten,* the sun, sometimes each of the rays held an *ankh* or tiny hands signifying that the sole god grants life and love not just to one individual, but to all people.

COMPLAINTS! COMPLAINTS!

❀

As the recognized vassal state of Egypt, the kings of Mitannia sent letters to the head of the Egyptian empire. Akhenaton was expected to take action to correct these transgressions against the people of Mitannia. In some of his letters, the King of Babylonia sent messages to Akhenaten complaining that his brother, apparently a miner, didn't send him enough gold to pay for the expenses of running the kingdom and maintaining the temple compounds:

❀

"Now my brother has sent me only two mines of gold. But this is a very small amount: tell him to send as much as our father sent! And if he has little gold, send half of what our father sent! My work in the houses of the Gods (temples) is abundant,

and now I have begun an undertaking: Send much gold!"

◌⟨⟩◌

A "mine" refers to half a kilogram of gold. Apparently, the king's late father used to supply him with more gold, but the king's brother has become less generous. Such were some of the petty arguments Akhenaton's subjects couldn't resolve for themselves.

◌⟨⟩◌

There was a number of letters from some of the kings and mayors of the city-states in Mesopotamia, begging for help in keeping away the attacks of Hittites. Either Akhenaton decided not to aid them or was unable to do so. He sometimes sent these governors letters chiding them for excessive complaints. The Assyrian historian, William Moran, indicated that more than 380 letters were located at the city of Armana alone!

FOREIGN RELATIONS

❧

Because history seems to be quiet about a number of actionable responses to complaints about being attacked, some analysts have concluded that Akhenatonturned a deaf ear to the people's needs. They indicate that the reason for that was the fact that Akhenaton was obsessed with promoting monotheism. However, he did respond in the more serious cases. Akhenaton was furious when betrayal Asiru, a city mayor, killed another mayor, Rib-Hadda:

❧

"If for any reason whatsoever you prefer to do evil,
and if you plot evil and treacherous things, than
you, together with your entire family shall die by
the axe of the king."

❧

Akhenaton imprisoned Asiru for a year but released him when he got word that the Hittites were threatening Asiru's kingdom. The pharaoh wanted him to return and organize an effective defense against them. That turned out to be an unwise move. Asiru immediately allied himself with the Hittites and this important territory was ceded to them.

⚜

Assaults from the Hittites continued, and it may have been because Akhenaton realized that Mesopotamia was so far away from Egypt that it was difficult to administer. Often, when an empire expands too far, it is managerially impossible to control it, as happened in the case of the Roman empire.

⚜

In addition, it was recorded that Akhenaten became very ill and may not have been strong enough to spend his energies dealing with political difficulties throughout the entire kingdom. As result, Egypt only had control of their own country, Northern Nubia and the coastal areas of the Levant at the end of his reign.

TUTANKHAMUN (1336-1323 BC):
THE TEEN WITH TREASURES

৩৯৫৬

Tutankhamun was nine-years-old when he assumed the throne of Egypt. He wasn't a healthy child, as he had a cleft palate like his grandfather, Akhenaten. He also had scoliosis which is a spinal deformity, a deformed foot and Klippel-Feil syndrome. That disorder is a fusion of some of the vertebrae in the cervical region. Archeologists found a number of canes in his tomb indicating that this condition along with the scoliosis was quite severe. Other symptomology included evidence that he suffered from frequent bouts of malaria. A number of his deformities may be attributable to the fact that he was the child born of the incestuous union between Akhenaten and Akhenaten's sister. He had relations with her before he married Nefertiti.

৩৯৫৬

A broken thigh bone was also discovered when the mummy was unwrapped, possibly caused by an accident. Because the tomb was constructed in a hurry, the leg injury probably brought on an infection that resulted in an early death. He was only nineteen.

⟡

The location of Tutankhamun's tomb remained hidden for many years. It was even unknown to the ancients because they had erected huts on top of it to house the tomb builders.

"BORROWED" GOLDEN TREASURES

༺✦༻

Analysts have studied the artifacts in King Tut's tomb and determined that many of the items placed inside were taken from the tomb of his stepmother, Nefertiti. Because the male is considered of a higher rank than the female, this was acceptable. Tomb robbers of the ancient times may have raided King Tut's tomb, but took very little – mostly perishable items like perfumes. Among the treasures found intact:

- Golden face mask
- Gold coffin
- Archery bows and arrows
- A chalice
- Thrones
- Dagger
- Food
- Wine
- Sandals and underwear

RESTORATION OF AMON-RA

⚜

The people under Akhenaten, his father, had resented his elimination of the worship of multiple deities in favor of the sole god *"**Aten**."* To please the people and suit his own beliefs, King Tut reversed that and restored the country to the worship of multiple deities under *Amon-Ra.*

⚜

Tutankhamun also resurrected the worship of the sacred bull deity, *"**Hapi**."* Some of the sculptures in Egypt are beautiful statues of bulls and the stone carvings have a disc between their horns. *Hapi* signified strength, courage and protection. The disc, of course, represents *Ra,* the sun god.

RAMESES II: RAMESES THE GREAT (1279-1213 BC)

❦

A khenaten had neglected the defenses of the Mesopotamian and Syrian territories. The Egyptians defensive forces were back in Thebes, and no longer guarded the fortifications they had built. Due to their negligence, the Hittites again re-entered the land and annexed huge amounts of territory. Kadesh was a vital city, rich in wealth and a center of trade. When no tributes were forthcoming from Kadesh, Rameses realized the oversight and took action.

SECOND BATTLE OF KADESH
1274 BC

୬୬

Rameses' forces were divided into four divisions named after the Egyptian gods, *Amon, Ra, Ptah* and *Set*. When Rameses' forces moved North and entered the area, the Hittites sent out a spy whose job it was to deliberately misdirect the Egyptians. He did so, and led Ramses to believe that the Hittites were further to the West.

୬୬

Rameses prepared his troops based on that information, but then met up with his own scouts who revealed the fact that he was being misled. Quickly, he tried to re-organize his troops but was caught by surprise. He sent word to the *Set* troops to rush North along with the *Ptah* forces as he and his men rushed into battle. The *Ra* division was only slightly South of Ramses' *Amon* battalions. The Hittites then sent out their charioteers who split up the *Ra* forces and they had to retreat. Then, only Ramses and his *Amon* force was left. They fought valiantly. According to the Egyptian script it said:

❦

*"So in ambush there they lay, Northwest of Kadesh
town; And while these were in their lair, others
went forth south of Kadesh in our midst. Their
charge was thrown with such weight that our
men went down. They took us unaware."*

❦

Next, the Hittites moved into the Egyptian encampment in order to plunder it for supplies. Shortly thereafter, Rameses' Southern divisions, the *Set* and the *Ptah* arrived from the South, joined Rameses and they staged six defensive battles with the Hittite warriors. After these bloody assaults, the Hittites moved further toward the Orontes River. According to the ancient carving:

❦

*"For the sixth time, I (Rameses) charged them. Like
Baal in his strength on their rearward, lo! And I
killed them. None escaped me, and I slew and
slew and slew."*

❦

After Ramses combined with his Southern forces, they forced the Hittites to withdraw toward the River. Upon reaching the banks, the desperate Hittites abandoned their chariots and attempted to swim across. Many drowned, and the rest surrendered.

PEACE TREATY BETWEEN THE
HITTITES AND EGYPT

வௐ

R ameses had to wage further campaigns against the
Hittites and their allies, the Hatti, who occupied
lands that lay further to the East. After a number of
years, the smaller kingdoms stopped rebelling because they
had lost so many men. A peace treaty was then drawn up. The
terms weren't as strong as those exerted by Tuthmosis III,
but Rameses realized that is would be too ambitious a goal to
make the terms too stringent. The smaller Mesopotamian
kingdoms were stronger since the reign of Tuthmosis and
total Egyptian domination wouldn't be possible.

வௐ

He also knew that defending this wide swatch of territory
would be expensive and could deplete the Egyptian treasury.
However, having such a peace treaty carved in stone would
stand as sufficient proof that Rameses achieved victory over
the Hittites. Of course, it was greatly exaggerated, but that

was the kind of propaganda pharaohs distributed for the population. Belief is sometimes much stronger than actionable proof.

A stela was inscribed to praise Ramses II when he left the vanquished territory:

> *"When day had broken, he made to retreat the*
> *Asiatics. They all came bowing down to him, to*
> *his palace of life and satisfaction, Per-Rameses-*
> *Amon-the-Great of Victories."*

GREAT TEMPLE AT ABU SIMBEL

๛

C arved into the side of a mountain lies one of the most spectacular monuments of Ancient Egypt. It is reported to have taken twenty years to construct. Four colossal statues of Ramses on his throne are hewn into the rock – each one showing a glorious aspect of his impressive reign. In the center is a bas-relief of *Horus*, also called **"Ra-Harakhti,"** which is the deity who the pharaoh represents... like a

"god on earth."

Inside the mountain, there are also huge statues of Rameses chief wife, Nefertari, his mother, Mut-Tuy, and eight of his children. Images of this edifice are some of the most popular ones displayed. They truly reflect the glory that was Egypt.

❦ V ❧

THE RAPID END OF THE EGYPTIAN CIVILIZATION

COLLAPSE OF THE BRONZE AGE

❧

Rameses II was the last great pharaoh of Egypt. His reign took place at the very end of the Bronze Age. Bronze was made from copper and tin. Copper was plentiful in the Egyptian lands, but the Egyptians constantly had to search for tin. The Hittites, Egypt's chief enemies, started to use iron after they devised techniques for manufacturing it from iron ore. Bronze weapons had a tendency to break, while the iron weapons were much firmer. In addition, once that process was perfected, the Hittites and other nearby tribes discovered that it was far less expensive to make the iron weapons. Use of iron weapons gave the Hittites a much greater advantage in warfare.

CENTRALIZED GOVERNMENTS

❧

E gypt steadfastly maintained a centralized government either out of Memphis or Thebes throughout most of the dynasties. Yet that geographical area they laid claim to was massive. Although they appointed emissaries and/or governors in the local provinces and smaller kingdoms, there was no way to control them without having to go out physically and inspect the areas. Word about civil strife or the gathering of armies had to be sent via human messengers. The time differential allowed the various subkingdoms time to increase their firepower and control to the point that they presented a formidable challenge. In addition, the Egyptian government became very top-heavy. Less attention was paid to the farmlands and prosperity of the people themselves. Simultaneously, the population was increasing at an exponential rate. Caravans were frequently attacked by bandits depriving Egypt of needed supplies and negatively impacted their economy.

VOLCANIC ERUPTION

࿓

During the 2^(nd) millennium BC, a powerful volcanic eruption took place on an island South of Greece. Even though there is quite distance from there to Egypt, the effects of an eruption can be far-reaching. It produces a cooling effect, which in turn, results in heavy crop losses. Ash clouds can travel thousands of miles and block out the sun's rays. In 1999, Frank Yurco cites it as a major cause of the collapse of Ancient Egypt.

DROUGHT

From their studies of the sediment layers built up over time, geophycists discovered that the civilizations in the Eastern Mediterranean and North Africa showed definitive evidence of a period of widespread drought. Soil samples were also taken from the Levant, just North East of Egypt, and they confirm the fact that there were more droughts that occurred at the end of the Bronze Age. That was a causative factor in the decline of the Egyptian civilization.

THE SEA PEOPLE

꧁꧂

I n Chapter 2, the rise of the "Sea People" was briefly addressed. Their historic origin is unknown, but it is believed that they were an alliance of people from Southern Europe, Asia Minor, the islands in the Mediterranean and Aegean Sea. They engaged in piracy regularly. For centuries they regularly raided the ships at sea, but started to disembark at the coastal countries surrounding the Eastern Mediterranean. This factor was noted in the hieroglyphic scripts during the reign of Rameses III, pharaoh circa 1186-1155 BC.

THE INTRUDERS WERE MORE
ADVANCED

৩৯৯

As the great empire of Ancient Egypt starting waning, in came more new conquerors – the Libyans, the Persians and then Alexander the Great. Although the conquerors marveled at the former beauty of the collapsing Egyptian monuments, they winced when they saw these Egyptian priests worshipping the crumbling statues of their old and silent animal gods. The conquerors considered these Egyptians primitive and mocked them when they saw the old Egyptian priests utter prayers to broken stone.

❦ VI ❦
CONCLUSION

❦

And there it lies – Egypt – in the desert sands of North Africa inundated by the luscious Nile during its seasons. The Egyptian Civilization emerged, thrived and fell, having weathered through thirty centuries. Ancient Egypt left an indelible mark on the history of this great green planet. It was a time of belief and a people bonded by those beliefs. It was a time of mighty satraps and pageantry never since repeated. Egypt reached its apex but has resurrected anew because of the never-ending interest in its philosophy, its art, its knowledge and its architecture. Ancient Egypt is alive today, not merely as something remembered, but as something that can be seen, touched and felt. Like its god, *Osiris,* it lives again.

❦

In these pages, you can see the mistakes the Ancient Egyptians made, but none that looms so large it would cause a civilization to curl up and die. Yet, it did.

YOUR FREE EBOOK!

As a way of saying thank you for reading our book, we're offering you a free copy of the below eBook.

Happy Reading!

Made in the USA
Middletown, DE
30 November 2018